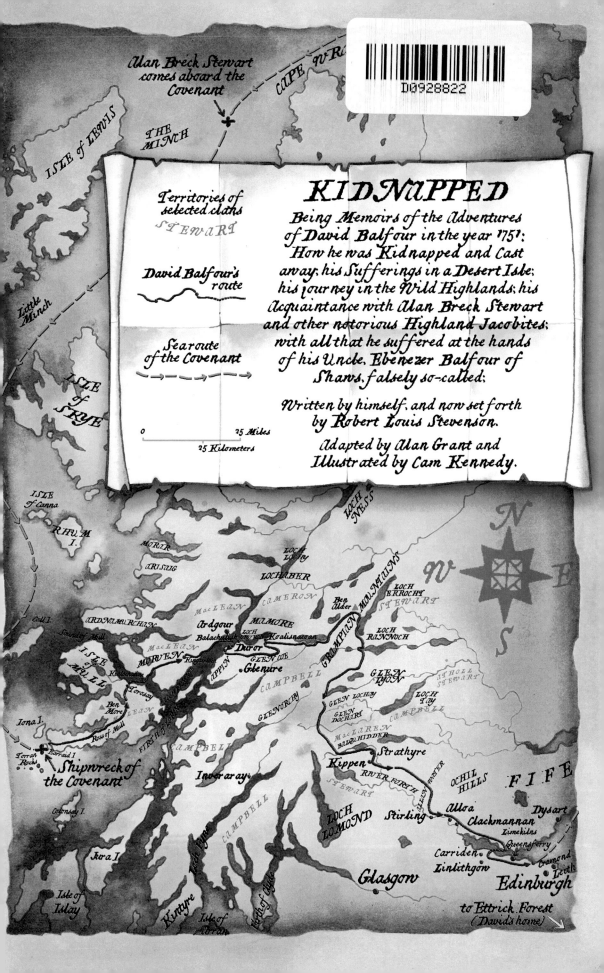

Alan Breck Stewart comes aboard the Covenant

CAPE WR...

THE MINCH

ISLE of LEWIS

Territories of selected clans
STEWART

David Balfour's route

Sea route of the Covenant

Little Minch

ISLE of SKYE

0   25 Miles
25 Kilometers

KIDNAPPED

Being Memoirs of the Adventures of David Balfour in the year 1751: How he was Kidnapped and Cast away; his Sufferings in a Desert Isle; his journey in the Wild Highlands; his Acquaintance with Alan Breck Stewart and other notorious Highland Jacobites; with all that he suffered at the hands of his Uncle, Ebenezer Balfour of Shaws, falsely so-called;

Written by himself, and now set forth by Robert Louis Stevenson.

Adapted by Alan Grant and Illustrated by Cam Kennedy.

LOCH NESS

ISLE of Canna

RHUM I.

MORAR

ARISAIG

LOCHABER

CAMERON

LOCH LOCHY

LOCH ERROCHT
STEWART

Ben Alder

GRAMPIAN MOUNTAINS

N
W E
S

Coll I.

ARDNAMURCHAN

MacLEAN

Ardgour

MILMORE

Balachulish

LOCH LEVEN

Koalisnacoan

LOCH RANNOCH

Sound of Mull

ISLE of MULL

MacLEAN

MORVEN

Kingairloch

Duror

GLEN COE

Glenure

APPIN

CAMPBELL

GLEN LYON

ATHOLL STEWART

Kinlochaline

Torosay

Ben More

LEAN

GLENIRCH

GLEN LOCHY

GLEN DOCHART

LOCH TAY

CAMPBELL

Iona I.

Ross of Mull

FIRST of LORNE

CAMPBELL

MacLAREN
BALQUHIDDER

Erraid I.

Torran Rocks

Shipwreck of the Covenant

Inveraray

Strathyre

Kippen

RIVER FORTH

OCHIL HILLS

FIFE

STEWART

Oronsay I.

CAMPBELL

LOCH LOMOND

Stirling

Alloa

Clackmannan

Dysart

Jura I.

Limekilns

Queensferry

Carriden
Linlithgow

Cramond
Leith

Isle of Islay

Kintyre

Isle of Arran

Forth of Clyde

Loch Fyne

Glasgow

Edinburgh

to Ettrick Forest
(David's home)

MY HEART BEAT HARD AT THIS GREAT PROSPECT SUDDENLY OPENING BEFORE A LAD OF SEVENTEEN...

IF YOU WERE IN MY SHOES, SIR, WOULD *YOU* GO?

THAT WOULD I, AND WITHOUT PAUSE!

THEN I WAS ALONE, OVERJOYED TO GET OUT OF THAT QUIET COUNTRYSIDE, AND GO TO A GREAT, BUSY HOUSE AMONG RICH AND RESPECTED GENTLEFOLK...

I TOOK MY LAST LOOK AT ESSENDEAN, AND THE BIG ROWANS IN THE KIRKYARD WHERE MY FATHER AND MY MOTHER LAY...

AND SET OUT FOR SHAWS, IN *CRAMOND*...

TO MEET MY UNKNOWN - AND WEALTHY! - RELATIVE.

ON THE FORENOON OF THE SECOND DAY, COMING TO THE TOP OF A HILL, I SAW ALL THE COUNTRY FALL AWAY BEFORE ME DOWN TO THE SEA; AND IN THE MIDST OF THIS DESCENT, ON A LONG RIDGE, THE **CITY** OF **EDINBURGH** SMOKING LIKE A KILN.

THERE WAS A FLAG UPON THE **CASTLE**, AND **SHIPS** LYING ANCHORED IN THE FIRTH; BOTH OF WHICH I COULD DISTINGUISH CLEARLY, AND BOTH BROUGHT MY COUNTRY HEART INTO MY MOUTH.

AROUND SUNDOWN I MET A SOUR-LOOKING WOMAN...

THAT IS THE HOUSE OF SHAWS! *BLOOD* BUILT IT... BLOOD *STOPPED* THE BUILDING OF IT...

AND *BLOOD* SHALL BRING IT *DOWN!*

IF YE SEE THE *LAIRD*, TELL HIM *JENNET CLOUSTON* CALLS DOWN A *CURSE* ON HIM AND HIS HOUSE!

BLACK, BLACK BE THEIR *FALL!*

I CARRIED MY FATHER'S LETTER, AND I WOULD NOT BE STOPPED. BUT I COULD NOT HELP BUT WONDER:

WAS *THIS* THE *PALACE* I HAD BEEN COMING TO?

WAS IT WITHIN *THESE* WALLS THAT I WAS TO SEEK NEW *FRIENDS* AND BEGIN *GREAT FORTUNES?*

THE LIGHT FROM A **FIRE** FLICKERED IN THE WINDOWS, BUT AT FIRST MY FRANTIC **KNOCKING** WENT UNHEEDED...

EBENEZER BALFOUR! I HAVE SOMETHING FOR YOU!

BE OFF WITH YE! THIS **BLUNDERBUSS** IS **LOADED!**

I CARRY A LETTER OF INTRODUCTION.

MY NAME IS **DAVID BALFOUR.**

IS YOUR FATHER DEAD?

AYE, HE'LL BE **DEAD,** AND THAT'LL BE WHAT BRINGS YE CHAPPING ON **MY** DOOR.

GO INTO THE KITCHEN — AND TOUCH **NAETHING!**

IT WAS THE BAREST ROOM I EVER SET MY EYES ON. THE TABLE WAS LAID FOR **SUPPER** WITH A BOWL OF **PORRIDGE**, A HORN SPOON AND A CUP OF **ALE**...

GIVE ME ALEXANDER'S LETTER.

YOU KNOW MY FATHER'S NAME?

IT WOULD BE STRANGE IF I DIDNAE. FOR HE WAS MY **BROTHER**.

SO YOU SEE, DAVIE MY MAN, I AM YOUR BORN **UNCLE**!

I WAS ASTONISHED, FOR MY FATHER HAD NEVER MENTIONED HE HAD A BROTHER. I SAT AND SUPPED THE MEAGRE BOWL OF PORRIDGE HE OFFERED, WHILE HE READ THE LETTER...

YE'LL HAVE HAD SOME **HOPES**, I'LL WAGER, OF **RICH KIN**?

I AM NO **BEGGAR**. I LOOK FOR NO FAVOURS.

HOOT-TOOT! DINNAE GET HUFFY WITH ME, DAVIE. WE'LL AGREE JUST FINE. NOW COME AWA' TO YOUR BED...

CAN I NOT HAVE A **LIGHT**, UNCLE?

LIGHTS IN A HOUSE IS A THING I DINNAE AGREE WITH, DAVIE. I'M A-FEARED OF **FIRES**, YE SEE.

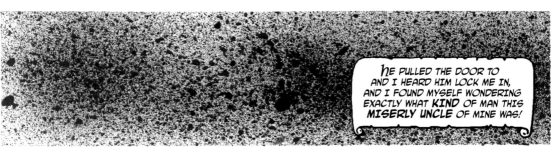

ᕼE PULLED THE DOOR TO AND I HEARD HIM LOCK ME IN, AND I FOUND MYSELF WONDERING EXACTLY WHAT **KIND** OF MAN THIS **MISERLY UNCLE** OF MINE WAS!

BY THE LIGHT OF THE DAWN, I SAW THAT TEN, OR PERHAPS TWENTY YEARS AGO, THIS MUST HAVE BEEN AS *PLEASANT* A ROOM AS A MAN COULD WISH.

BUT TIME, AND SEVERE NEGLECT, HAD DONE THEIR WORST.

MY UNCLE'S DIET SEEMED TO CONSIST ONLY OF PORRIDGE AND WEAK BEER...

IT IS OBVIOUS YOU DO NOT WANT ME HERE, SIR. FAMILY OR NOT, IT MIGHT BE BETTER IF I LEAVE.

HOOTS-TOOTS! CA' CANNIE, DAVIE! BIDE A DAY OR TWO... I'LL DO THE RIGHT THING BY YOU, YOU'LL SEE.

I PASSED SOME TIME IN THE OLD LIBRARY...

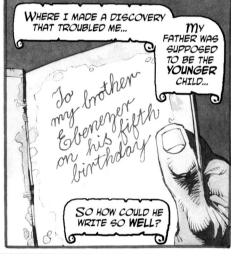

WHERE I MADE A DISCOVERY THAT TROUBLED ME... MY FATHER WAS SUPPOSED TO BE THE *YOUNGER* CHILD...

To my brother Ebenezer on his fifth birthday

SO HOW COULD HE WRITE SO *WELL*?

WHEN I ASKED MY UNCLE ABOUT IT...

WERE YOU AND MY FATHER *TWINS*, BY ANY CHANCE?

EH? EH?

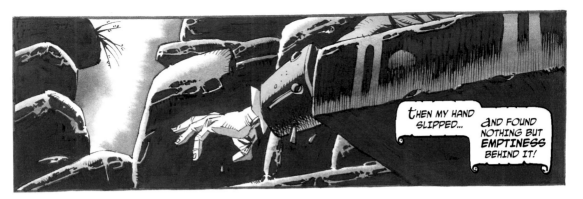

THEN MY HAND SLIPPED... AND FOUND NOTHING BUT **EMPTINESS** BEHIND IT!

THE MERE THOUGHT OF THE PERIL IN WHICH I STOOD, AND THE DREADFUL HEIGHT I MIGHT HAVE FALLEN FROM, BROUGHT OUT THE SWEAT UPON MY BODY.

FOR THE STAIR HAD BEEN BUILT NO HIGHER. ONE MORE STEP WOULD HAVE SENT ME CRASHING TO MY **DOOM!**

MY UNCLE IS TRYING TO **KILL** ME!

HE SENT ME HERE TO **DIE!**

ANGER BURNED IN MY HEART AS I GROPED MY WAY DOWN. BY THE TIME I REACHED GROUND, THE STORM HAD BROKEN...

THERE HE IS - LISTENING FOR THE SOUND OF MY FALL!

THERE WAS A GREAT TOW-ROW OF **THUNDER**. MY UNCLE WAS SEIZED BY A KIND OF PANIC FEAR AND RAN INSIDE...

I CAME CLOSE BEHIND HIM, AND SUDDENLY CLAPPED MY HANDS UPON HIS SHOULDERS...

AH-**HA**!

AIIEEEE!

D-D-DAVIE! ARE YE ALIVE? O, MAN, ARE YE ALIVE?

THAT I AM - SMALL THANKS TO YOU!

WHY GIVE ME **MONEY** - THEN TRY TO **KILL** ME? WHY DO YOU **FEAR** ME SO?

I-I'LL TELL YE EVERYTHING, DAVIE. IN THE MORNING.

IT'S MY **HEART**, YE SEE. I'M FEELING UNCO **WEAK**!

I LOCKED HIM IN HIS ROOM, AND MADE UP SUCH A **BLAZE** AS HAD NOT SHONE IN THAT KITCHEN FOR MANY A LONG YEAR.

DEEP INTO THE NIGHT, I SAT THERE, AND PONDERED ON THE MYSTERY OF THIS RUINED **HOUSE** OF SHAWS.

NEXT MORNING, I URGED HIM TO ANSWER ME. BUT...

HIS ATTEMPTS TO THINK UP SOME CUNNING *LIE* WERE INTERRUPTED BY A KNOCKING AT THE DOOR...

HOOT-TOOT, *DAVIE!* LET ME FINISH MY *PARRITCH!*

YOU STAY WHERE YOU ARE, SIR. I WILL SEE TO IT.

WHAT CHEER, MATE?

I'VE BROUGHT A LETTER FROM OLD *HEASY-OASY* TO MR BELFLOWER.

AN' I SAY, MATE - I'M *HUNGRY.*

MORTAL HUNGRY!

LISTEN TO THIS, DAVIE!

MY PARTNER, **CAPTAIN HOSEASON,** REQUIRES MY PRESENCE AT THE **QUEEN'S FERRY.**

IF YE COME WITH ME, WE CAN VISIT WITH THE LAWYER, **RANKEILLOR.** HE WAS A **FRIEND** OF YOUR **FATHER'S.**

MY UNCLE WOULD HARDLY DARE *VIOLENCE* AGAINST ME AT A BUSY *HARBOUR.* AND I WAS EAGER TO MEET A MAN OF THE LAW, MOREOVER ONE WHO KNEW MY FATHER...

VERY WELL.

LET US GO!

THEY CALLS ME **RANSOME**, MATE.

I BEEN A SALTY SEA-DOG SINCE I WERE ONLY A LITTL'UN.

CAPTAIN HEASY-OASY'S A HARD MAN, BUT HE AIN'T NO SAILOR. MR **SHUAN'S** CHIEF MATE, AN' HE SAILS THE BOAT.

BUT WHEN HE'S **DRUNK**, HE **BEATS** ME SOMETHIN' AWFUL!

HE'LL BE **SORRY** ONE DAY, YOU SEE IF HE AIN'T!

I'VE KILLED A MAN AFORE, YE KNOW. AYE, **MORE** THAN ONE!

BUT THERE'S WORSE OFF THAN ME.

THERE'S THE **TWENTY-POUNDERS** – MEN **KIDNAPPED** TO BE SOLD AS **SLAVES** IN THE COTTON FIELDS OF **AMERICA!**

SHORTLY, *CAPTAIN HOSEASON* HIMSELF CAME TO SEE ME...

YOUR UNCLE TELLS ME GREAT THINGS OF YOU, DAVID. YE SHALL COME ON BOARD MY SHIP, AND DRINK A BOWL.

I AM SORRY, CAPTAIN. BUT I MUST SEE RANKEILLOR, THE LAWYER.

TAKE CARE, LAD. YOUR UNCLE MEANS TO DO YOU HARM!

COME ABOARD MY BOAT UNTIL I CAN HAVE A PRIVATE WORD WITH YOU!

I THOUGHT I HAD FOUND A *FRIEND*, SOMEONE WHO WOULD *HELP* ME IN MY DIFFICULTY.

SO, LIKE A FOOL, I WENT WILLINGLY TO MY FATE...

THE CAPTAIN AND I WERE FIRST TO BE HOIST ABOARD...

BUT WHERE IS MY UNCLE?

AYE, LAD. THAT'S THE POINT!

THE SKIFF WAS HEADING BACK TO SHORE...

I'VE BEEN TRICKED!

HELP! HELP!

MY UNCLE'S FACE WAS FULL OF CRUELTY AND TERROR...

STRONG HANDS GRABBED ME AND PULLED ME AWAY...

I SAW A GREAT FLASH OF FIRE AS A THUNDERBOLT SEEMED TO STRIKE ME...

AND I FELL SENSELESS TO THE DECK.

I CAME TO IN DARKNESS, IN GREAT PAIN. THE WHOLE WORLD HEAVED GIDDILY UP AND DOWN, AND I HEARD THE **ROARING** OF WATER AND THE SHRILL **CRIES** OF SEAMEN...

IT TOOK ME A LONG WHILE TO REALISE I MUST BE LYING SOMEWHERE IN THE BELLY OF THAT UNLUCKY SHIP, AND THAT WE WERE PLOUGHING THROUGH A **GALE**.

THERE FELL ON ME A BLACKNESS OF **DESPAIR**, A HORROR OF **REMORSE** AT MY OWN FOLLY, AND A PASSION OF **ANGER** AT MY TRAITOROUS UNCLE.

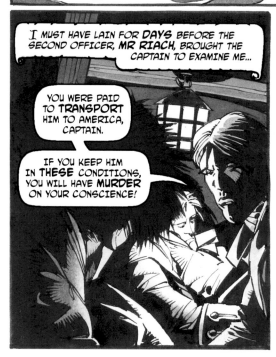

I MUST HAVE LAIN FOR **DAYS** BEFORE THE SECOND OFFICER, **MR RIACH**, BROUGHT THE CAPTAIN TO EXAMINE ME...

YOU WERE PAID TO **TRANSPORT** HIM TO AMERICA, CAPTAIN.

IF YOU KEEP HIM IN **THESE** CONDITIONS, YOU WILL HAVE **MURDER** ON YOUR CONSCIENCE!

I WAS PUT IN THE **FORECASTLE** WITH THE OTHER MEN, AND HERE I STAYED RECOVERING.

THEY WERE A ROUGH LOT, AS SAILORS MOSTLY ARE. SOME AMONG THEM HAD SAILED WITH **PIRATES**, WHILE OTHERS WERE **DESERTERS** FROM KING GEORGE'S **NAVY**.

BUT, FOR THE MOST PART, THEY WERE NOT EVIL – WITH THE EXCEPTION PERHAPS OF THE DRUNKEN **MR SHUAN**...

YE SCURVY BRAT! YE DESERVE A GOOD WALLOPIN'!

BUT SHUAN WAS THE ONLY **TRUE SAILOR** AMONGST THE WHOLE JING-BANG.

THEY **NEEDED** HIS KNOWLEDGE, AND SO NONE WOULD BE CRITICAL.

I TRIED TO BEFRIEND RANSOME, BUT TRUTH BE TOLD, HIS MIND WAS SCARCELY HUMAN...

OH 'TIS MY DELIGHT ON A SHINY NIGHT IN THE SEASON OF THE YEAR!

DON'T REMEMBER ME FATHER. HE MADE CLOCKS, I FINK. WE HAD A **STARLIN'**, SEE, THAT COULD WHISTLE RIGHT PRETTY.

DON'T YOU WANT TO **FIND** YOUR FATHER? TO GO **HOME**?

THIS BE MY HOME NOW – THE **SEA**, AN' THE **WIND**, AN' ME PANNIKIN OF **ALE**!

ALL THIS TIME, THE SHIP WAS MEETING CONSTANT HEADWINDS AND ROUGH SEA, MEANING HARD LABOUR FOR ALL HANDS.

MORE THAN A **WEEK** WENT BY, AND MY HEART SANK LOWER AND LOWER.

THE SHADOW OF POOR **RANSOME** LAY HEAVILY ON ME, AND STILL I WAS BOUND FOR **SLAVERY.** EVEN THE SHIP ITSELF SEEMED CURSED WITH **ILL LUCK**...

ON THE TENTH NIGHT THERE WAS A TERRIBLE **SHRIEK** OF TORTURED WOOD AND THE SOUND OF **DESPERATE CRIES**...

FOR PITY'S SAKE! THEY'VE RUN US DOWN!

THERE'S A SURVIVOR!

THROW HIM A LINE AND WE'LL SAVE HIM YET!

THE CAPTAIN WENT OUT - HURRIEDLY, I THOUGHT - AND LEFT ME ALONE WITH THE STRANGER...

SO...YOU ARE A **REBEL**, SIR?

AYE. AND YOU, BY YOUR LONG FACE, ARE A **WHIG**.

WELL, MR WHIG - THIS BOTTLE IS **DRY**.

IT'S NOT EASY TO PAY SIXTY GUINEAS, AND BE **GRUDGED** A WEE **DRAM**!

I WILL ASK THE CAPTAIN FOR MORE.

I HEARD MUFFLED VOICES IN THE FOG...

WE CAN FALL ONE UPON EACH SIDE OF HIM, AND PIN HIM BY THE ARMS!

WE CAN STAB HIM BEFORE HE HAS TIME TO DRAW!

DAVID! YON WILD HIELANDMAN IS A **DANGER** TO THE SHIP AND AN **ENEMY** OF OUR KING!

YOU MUST GET US THE **FIREARMS** FROM THE ROUNDHOUSE... AND WE WILL **SHARE** HIS **GOLD** WITH YOU!

VERY WELL, SIRS.

I WILL DO IT.

BUT I WAS SEIZED WITH **ANGER** AT THESE TREACHEROUS, GREEDY, BLOODY MEN - AND I KNEW I COULD NOT DO IT!

DO YE WANT TO BE KILLED, JACOBITE?

EH? WHAT'S THIS YE SAY?

THEY'RE ALL MURDERERS HERE! THEY'VE KILLED A BOY ALREADY - AND NOW IT'S YOU!

AYE, AYE... BUT THEY HAVEN'T GOT ME YET.

WILL YE STAND WITH ME, LAD?

I AM NO THIEF, NOR YET MURDERER! I'LL STAND BY YOU. I AM DAVID BALFOUR.

OF SHAWS.

MY NAME IS STEWART - A KING'S NAME. BUT THEY CALL ME ALAN BRECK.

WE DOLED OUT CUTLASSES AND PISTOLS FROM THE STORE...

THERE ARE FIFTEEN AGAINST US!

I WILL GUARD THE MAIN DOOR, DAVID. YOU MUST TAKE THE REST!

I WARN YOU, ALAN BRECK - I AM NO GREAT SHOT!

THEN DINNAE FIRE TO THIS SIDE - FOR I WOULD RATHER HAVE TEN FOES IN FRONT OF ME, THAN ONE FRIEND LIKE YOU CRACKING PISTOLS AT MY BACK!

TAKE THAT!

I HAD NEVER FIRED A PISTOL IN MY LIFE, BUT IT WAS NOW OR NEVER...

THEY BROKE AND RAN...

WHILE INSIDE, ALAN BRECK'S SWORD RAN RED WITH BLOOD.

I WOUNDED AT LEAST ONE OF THEM!

AND I HAVE SETTLED TWO.

BUT THAT'S NOT ENOUGH BLOOD, DAVID BALFOUR...

THIS WAS BUT A DRAM BEFORE THE MEAT.

THEY WILL BE BACK IN FORCE!

ALAN CAME UP TO ME WITH OPEN ARMS, AND EMBRACED ME...

DAVID, LAD - I LOVE YE LIKE A **BROTHER!**

AND O, MAN, AM I NO' A BONNIE FIGHTER?

MR SHUAN AND FIVE MORE WERE KILLED OUTRIGHT, AND FOUR MORE WERE HURT...

ALL OF A SUDDEN, I BEGAN TO **CRY** LIKE ANY CHILD...

HUSH, DAVID. YE ARE A BRAW LAD. IT TAKES MUCH TO KILL A MAN, FOR IT GOES AGAINST HUMAN NATURE!

I HAD THESE **BUTTONS** FROM MY FATHER, DUNCAN.

I GIVE ONE OF THEM TO YOU, DAVID, A **KEEPSAKE** FOR THIS NIGHT'S BLOODY WORK.

WHEREVER YE GO AND SHOW THAT BUTTON, THE FRIENDS OF ALAN BRECK WILL COME TO AID YOU!

COME MORNING, THE CAPTAIN HAD NO CHOICE BUT TO NEGOTIATE...

YE'VE MADE A RIGHT HASH OF MY BRIG, SIR!

YOUR OWN FAULT, CAPTAIN. A GENTLEMAN SHOULD ALWAYS KEEP HIS WORD.

IN A FEW HOURS' TIME, I CAN SET YOU ASHORE AT ARDNAMURCHAN.

CAMPBELL COUNTRY?

OH NO, SIR. I'M A STEWART, AND THE CAMPBELLS ARE MY SWORN ENEMY!

IF YE WANT YOUR SIXTY GUINEAS, THE LINNHE LOCH IT IS!

AS WE SAILED THROUGH THE LITTLE MINCH PAST THE ISLE OF CANNA, I LEARNED MORE OF ALAN BRECK AND HIS HATRED OF CLAN CAMPBELL.

COLIN ROY IS THE WORST - THE MAN CALLED THE RED FOX!

THE RED FOX IS KING GEORGE'S AGENT IN MY CLAN'S LANDS. HE DRIVES OUT MY KINSMEN, AND TRANSPORTS THEM TO THE COLONIES! HE USES EVERY TRICK TO STEAL OUR LAND, AND OUR MONEY!

I TELL YE THIS, DAVID...

IF I LAY DYING, I WOULD CRAWL UPON MY KNEES TO FIRE ONE LAST SHOT AT THE RED FOX!

THE COVENANT SORELY MISSED MR SHUAN'S SKILLS IN NAVIGATION.

WE WERE SOMEWHERE OFF THE COAST OF MULL WHEN...

REEF! REEF ON THE LEE BOW!

THE TORRAN ROCKS, THEY CALL THEM. ABOUT TEN MILES LONG, BY ALL ACCOUNTS!

WE HAVE NO CHOICE BUT TO CHANCE THEM!

NEXT MOMENT WE STRUCK THE REEF WITH A DUNCH THAT THREW US FLAT ON THE DECK...

ALAN! HELP ME LOOSE THE SKIFF AND WE MAY YET LIVE!

FOR WHAT? THOSE ARE THE ISLANDS OF *EARRAID* AND *MULL*... CAMPBELL COUNTRY! I AM A DEAD MAN THERE!

OF A SUDDEN, A HUGE SWELL THREW THE BRIG OVER. I LOST MY HOLD, AND WAS CAST CLEAN OVER THE BULWARKS INTO THE SEA...

FOR PITY'S SAKE!

DAVID!

I CLUTCHED DESPERATELY AT A BROKEN SPAR...

HELP!

HELP!

BUT THE *COVENANT* WAS GONE.

ᴀs I WAS WASHED ASHORE, I THOUGHT IN MY HEART I HAD NEVER SEEN A PLACE SO *DESERTED* AND *DESOLATE* AS THIS ISLAND OF *EARRAID*.

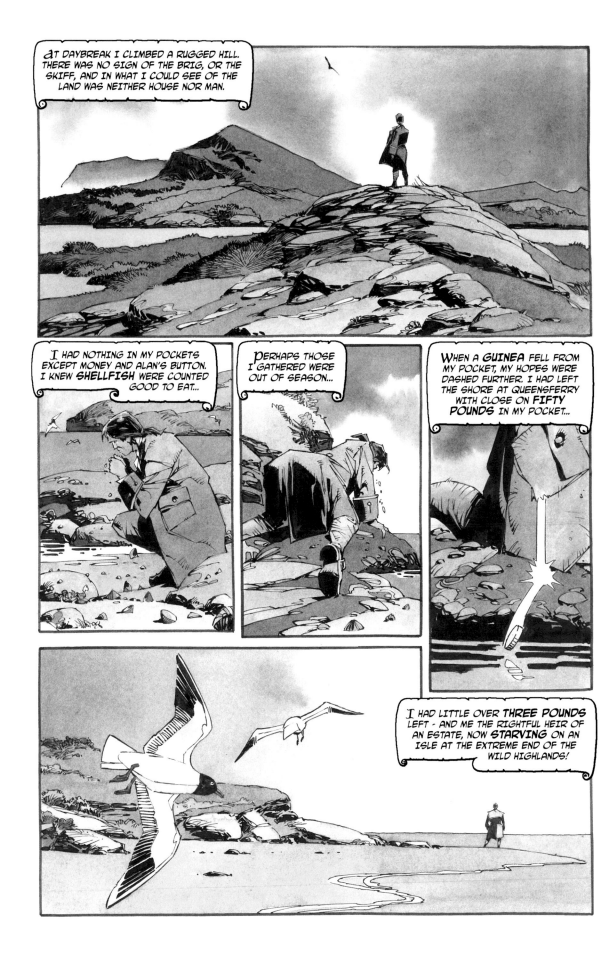

NEXT MORNING...

WHICH WAY TO TOROSAY, MY FRIEND?

NAE ENGLISH! GO AWAY! NAE ENGLISH!

SO I LET MY **MONEY** SPEAK FOR ME...

AND SUDDENLY, HE FOUND HIS TONGUE...

TOROSAY?

OCH AYE, IT'S NO' SAE FAR AT ALL, AT ALL. I'LL JUST TAK' YE THERE MYSEL', AND IT'LL ONLY COST YE **FIVE SHILLINGS!**

WE WALKED FOR MILES IN SILENCE, UNTIL...

I'LL BE NEEDING FIVE SHILLINGS **MORE** NOO - OR YE CAN FIND YER AIN WAY!

WHY, YOU IMPUDENT, CHEATING RUFFIAN!

YE'LL PAY UP, BY HOOK OR BY CROOK!

BUT I WAS A STRONG LAD, AND VERY ANGRY...

PERHAPS, SIR, THAT WILL TEACH YOU TO KEEP YOUR WORD IN THE FUTURE!

IT TOOK ME **FOUR DAYS** FROM EARRAID TO TOROSAY, A DISTANCE OF SOME FIFTY MILES. BUT AT LAST I SAT IN THE FERRY OF ALAN BRECK'S KINSMAN, NEIL ROY McROB...

IN THE MOUTH OF LOCH ALINE, WE FOUND A GREAT BOAT AT ANCHOR, AN **EMIGRANT** SHIP BOUND FOR THE AMERICAN **COLONIES**.

WHEN MEN LIKE THE **RED FOX** COULD GET NO RENT FROM THE PEOPLE, THEY OFTEN **STOLE** THEIR LANDS, AND **SOLD** THE HAPLESS FAMILIES INTO **BONDAGE**.

IN ALL MY FURTHEST JOURNEYINGS, I SWEAR I NEVER SAW SUCH A CRUEL AND HEART-PIERCING SIGHT.

ON LAND ONCE MORE, I SHOWED MY **SILVER BUTTON** TO NEIL ROY...

ALAN SAID YOU WOULD COME. HE HAS LEFT INSTRUCTIONS.

ALAN HAD LEFT A ROUTE FOR ME TO FOLLOW: I WAS TO REACH **ARDGOUR** THE NEXT DAY, AND SPEND THE NIGHT IN THE HOME OF **JOHN OF THE CLAYMORE.**

TWO DAYS LATER I WOULD CROSS THE LOCH AT **BALACHULISH,** THEN FIND MY WAY TO **JAMES OF THE GLENS** AT AUCHARN IN APPIN.

SO, AT LAST, I FOUND MYSELF IN **APPIN,** CLOSE TO THE WOOD OF **LETTERMORE...**

IT WAS HERE THAT I WAS DOUBLY ASSAILED, NOT ONLY BY A CLOUD OF STINGING **MIDGES...**

BUT WORSE, BY THE **DOUBTS** OF MY OWN **MIND.** WHY WAS I TRACING THE FOOTSTEPS OF AN **OUTLAW,** ALAN BRECK? WHY HAD I NOT SET OUT ON MY OWN, HEADING SOUTH AND EAST FOR **EDINBURGH?**

HAD I **LOST** ALL MY **SENSE?**

HURRY! WE CAN CATCH HIM YET!

THAT LAD IS AN **ACCOMPLICE**! TEN POUNDS TO THE MAN WHO SHOOTS HIM **DEAD**!

FIRELOCKS BANGED, AND THE BALLS WHISTLED IN THE BIRCHES, AND MY HEART CAME INTO MY MOUTH WITH **TERROR**.

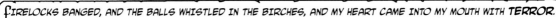

THIS WAS NOT THE WAY IT SHOULD BE!

YOU HEARD THE LAWYER. TEN POUNDS FOR HIS LIFE!

I RAN FOR ALL I WAS WORTH...

UNTIL, MOST ASTONISHINGLY, I HEARD A VOICE...

JOUK IN HERE AMONG THE BUSHES!

ALAN!

ALAN BRECK!

IT IS NO TIME FOR CIVILITIES, DAVIE.

FOR YOUR LIFE, LAD - FOLLOW ME!

THE PACE WAS DEADLY, AND MY HEART SEEMED LIKE IT WOULD BURST AGAINST MY RIBS. BUT ALAN DID NOT SLACKEN, AND I FORCED MYSELF TO STAY WITH HIM.

AT LAST, HIGH IN THE WOOD, WE RESTED IN THE BRACKEN, AND I COULD VOICE THE THOUGHTS THAT TROUBLED ME...

I LIKED YOU VERY WELL, ALAN - BUT I CAN HAVE NO PART IN COLD-BLOODED MURDER!

AS ONE FRIEND TO ANOTHER, MR BALFOUR OF SHAWS...

IF I WERE GOING TO KILL A GENTLEMAN, I WOULD NOT DO IT IN MY OWN COUNTRY, TO BRING TROUBLE ON MY CLAN.

AND I WOULD TAKE A SWORD AND GUN - NOT A FISHING ROD ON MY BACK!

THEY'LL BE AFTER US BOTH NOW.

WE HAVE TO FLEE!

I HAVE NO FEAR OF THE JUSTICE OF MY OWN COUNTRY.

DAVIE, DAVIE! I WONDER AT YOUR INNOCENCE.

A CAMPBELL HAS BEEN KILLED. WE'LL BE TRIED IN INVERARA, THE CAMPBELL CAPITAL, WITH FIFTEEN CAMPBELLS ON THE JURY AND THEIR DUKE AS THE JUDGE.

WE'LL GET THE SAME JUSTICE THE RED FOX GOT AT THAT ROADSIDE!

EITHER TAKE TO THE HEATHER WITH ME - AN OUTLAW - OR HANG LIKE A DOG!

PUT LIKE THAT, ALAN, IT'S NO CHOICE AT ALL!

As we journeyed, Alan told me how the **COVENANT** had finally **SUNK**, and how he had escaped from Hoseason and the other survivors...

Alan had intended us to **HIDE OUT** at James of the Glens' home, but the murder of the Red Fox had **CHANGED** everything...

THE REDCOATS WILL BE **SWARMING** HERE TOMORROW! WE WILL NEED TO TRAVEL ON.

They fed us, and clothed us, but...

IT'S A SORRY BUSINESS, ALAN.

IF THEY SEEK **YOU**, THEY WILL SEEK **ME**. I HAVE ONLY ONE ESCAPE...

I MUST PUT OUT A **REWARD** UPON YOU!

Alan's **MONEY BELT** HAD BEEN SENT ON BY OTHER MEANS. SO, FURNISHED WITH SWORDS AND PISTOLS, OATMEAL AND BRANDY - WITH REWARDS UPON OUR OUTLAW HEADS! - WE WERE READY FOR **THE HEATHER.**

DAY FOUND US IN A PRODIGIOUS **VALLEY**, STREWN WITH ROCKS AND WHERE RAN A FOAMING RIVER. WILD MOUNTAINS STOOD AROUND IT; THERE GREW THERE NEITHER GRASS NOR TREES.

I HAVE SOMETIMES THOUGHT SINCE THEN THAT IT MAY HAVE BEEN THE VALLEY CALLED **GLENCOE**, WHERE THE **MASSACRE** HAD BEEN IN THE NAME OF KING WILLIAM.

IT WAS A BARREN AND AN EERIE PLACE, TRULY A GLEN OF SORROW.

AND IT IS THANKS ONLY TO PROVIDENCE WE WERE NOT A MOMENT TOO SOON...

COME NIGHT, WE'LL SLIP DOWN AND GET BY THEM.

AND WHAT ARE WE TO DO TILL NIGHT?

COOK, DAVIE. WE'RE GOING TO BAKE LIKE TATTIE SCONES IN THAT SUN!

He had come by copies of our **wanted** papers...

It says Alan Breck is "A small, pock-marked, active man dressed in French clothes" whose companion is "A tall strong lad, about eighteen, with no beard."

Despite food and drink I felt weak and **fevered**. I took to bed, while Alan and Cluny played **cards**...

I woke, and slept, and slept and woke, and all seemed to be some strange **dream**...

David - I need to borrow your money. All right, lad?

I... I suppose so...

When at last I felt recovered, it was only to find...

Ye shouldnae have given me your money, Davie! I'm **daft** when it comes to the cards!

I've **lost** the lot - aye, and my own gold, too!

To cut a sorry tale short, Cluny gave me back my share of the money, though very reluctantly.

When Alan and I left his cage, we could hardly bear to speak one with the other...

WE LAID UP FOR NEARLY A **MONTH** AT THE HOME OF A MacLAREN IN THE **BRAES OF BALQUHIDDER.** HERE A **DOCTOR** WAS FETCHED, WHO TENDED TO ME CONSTANTLY.

IT WAS FAR THROUGH **AUGUST** WHEN I RECOMMENCED MY JOURNEY. OUR MONEY WAS ALMOST GONE, SO IT WAS **IMPERATIVE** I FIND THE LAWYER **RANKEILLOR.**

THE **BRIDGE** AT **STIRLING** BEING WELL-GUARDED WITH **REDCOATS,** ALAN MANAGED TO ARRANGE FOR US TO TAKE A BOAT ACROSS THE WATERS...

AND AT LONG, LONG LAST I CAME HOME TO THE LOWLANDS.

IT WAS DECIDED ALAN WOULD HIDE NEAR NEWHALLS, WHILE I WENT TO THE **QUEEN'S FERRY** IN SEARCH OF MY UNCLE EBENEZER'S **LAWYER**, RANKEILLOR...

I TOLD HIM THE WHOLE STORY, FROM THE LEAVING OF **ESSENDEAN** TO MY JOURNEY THROUGH THE **HIGHLANDS**, LEAVING OUT NOTHING OF MY UNCLE'S **TREACHERY**...

TUT TUT! TO HAVE HIS OWN NEPHEW **KIDNAPPED!**

BUT WHEN I CAME TO MENTION **ALAN BRECK**...

I AM A MAN OF THE LAW, DAVID. I CANNOT COMPROMISE MY POSITION.

IF YOU **MUST** TALK OF OUTLAWS, THEN GIVE HIM ANOTHER **NAME**...

MR THOMSON, FOR INSTANCE.

SHAWS IS UNDOUBTEDLY **YOURS**, DAVID. BUT IF EBENEZER OBJECTS, IT WILL BE A HARD MATTER TO **PROVE**.

I THINK, SIR, THAT I MAY HAVE A **SCHEME** THAT WILL MAKE MY UNCLE **CONFESS** TO HIS MISDEEDS.

AND I SHALL NEED THE SERVICES OF MY FRIEND... MR THOMSON!

RANKEILLOR CAME WITH ME TO NEWHALLS, AND I WHISTLED THE **SIGNAL** THAT HAD BEEN AGREED...

WE TOLD ALAN - OR SHOULD I SAY, **MR THOMSON** - MY PLAN, AND ALL THREE OF US SET FORTH TO PLAY THE FINAL ACT...

NIGHT WAS FALLEN WHEN WE CAME IN VIEW OF THE HOUSE OF SHAWS. AS WE DREW NEAR, WE SAW NO GLIMMER OF LIGHT IN ANY PART OF THE BUILDING...

THE LAWYER AND I CREPT QUIETLY UP AND CROUCHED DOWN BESIDE THE CORNER OF THE HOUSE...

WHILE ALAN MARCHED UP AND BEGAN A THUND'ROUS KNOCKING ON THE DOOR...

EBENEZER BALFOUR! I WOULD HAVE **WORDS** WITH YOU!

THIS IS NAE TIME OF NIGHT FOR DECENT FOLK! WHAT BRINGS YE HERE?

I HAVE A **BLUNDERBUSS**, MIND!

I WOULD TALK ABOUT DAVID BALFOUR, SIR!

IT SEEMS A **SHIP** WENT DOWN OFF THE ISLE OF MULL, AND A **SURVIVOR** - THIS DAVID BALFOUR - FELL INTO THE HANDS OF MY KIN.

THEY HAVE HIM **PRISONER** IN AN AULD, RUINED CASTLE...

AND I FEAR THEY WILL DO HIM **ILL** UNLESS YOU HAVE **MONEY** TO **PAY** FOR HIM!

OCH, I'M NO' VERY CARING. HE WASNAE A GOOD LAD AT THE BEST OF IT, AND I'VE NAE CALL TO PAY A **RANSOM**!

HOOT, SIR! YE'RE A HARD MAN, TO DESERT YOUR OWN BROTHER'S SON!

SO...DO YE WANT HIM **KILLED** - OR **KEPT**?

KEPT, SIR, KEPT! I'LL NOT SANCTION MURDER!

AS FOR HOW MUCH, THEN - WHAT DID YE PAY **HOSEASON** TO **KIDNAP** THE LAD IN THE FIRST PLACE?

TWENTY POUNDS. AND HE'D HAVE GOT **ANOTHER** TWENTY WHEN HE **SOLD** THE BOY IN THE CAROLINAS!

THANK YOU, MR BALFOUR. A MOST **EXCELLENT** CONFESSION!

RANKEILLOR!

OH, MICHTY ME! D-D-**DAVID**!

GOOD EVENING, UNCLE!

COME COME, MR EBENEZER. DO NOT BE DOWNHEARTED. WE SHALL MAKE **EASY TERMS** WITH YOU, SIR!

ＡND THAT WE DID. EBENEZER AGREED TO PAY ME **TWO-THIRDS** OF THE YEARLY INCOME AT SHAWS. SO THE BEGGAR HAD COME HOME, AND NOW I WAS A **MAN OF MEANS** AND HAD A **NAME** IN THE COUNTRY.

NEXT DAY, ALAN AND I WENT SLOWLY FORWARD, HAVING LITTLE HEART EITHER TO WALK OR SPEAK. WE WERE NEAR THE TIME OF OUR **PARTING**, AND REMEMBRANCE OF ALL THE **BYGONE DAYS** SAT UPON US SORELY.

WE CAME THE BY-WAY OVER THE HILL OF **CORSTORPHINE**, AND LOOKED DOWN ON THE BOGS AND OVER TO THE CITY AND THE CASTLE ON THE HILL. AND WE KNEW WE HAD COME TO WHERE OUR WAYS PARTED.

IT WAS COMING NEAR NOON WHEN I PASSED IN BY THE **WEST KIRK** AND THE **GRASSMARKET** INTO THE STREETS OF THE CAPITAL, WHERE RANKEILLOR HAD PLACED A **CREDIT** THAT MIGHT TAKE ALAN TO **SAFETY** IN FRANCE...

tHE HUGE **HEIGHT** OF THE BUILDINGS, THE NARROW ARCHED **ENTRIES**, THE **HUBBUB** AND ENDLESS STIR... ALL STRUCK ME INTO A KIND OF **STUPOR** OF **SURPRISE**...

SO THAT I LET THE CROWD CARRY ME TO AND FRO.

YET ALL THE TIME WHAT I WAS THINKING OF WAS **ALAN** AT CORSTORPHINE.

aND ALL THE TIME THERE WAS A COLD **GNAWING** ON MY INSIDE, LIKE A **REMORSE** FOR SOMETHING **WRONG**.

THE HAND OF PROVIDENCE BROUGHT ME IN MY DRIFTING TO THE VERY DOOR OF THE **BRITISH LINEN COMPANY'S** BANK.

the end